BIOGRAPHY OF STEVE BALLMER

Life and Times of The Man Who
Revolutionized Tech Industry

Blake Hayden

Table Of Contents

Introduction

The Passionate Roar of a Tech Titan

In the vast and dynamic landscape of the technology world, certain figures leave an indelible mark that shapes the industry's trajectory for generations to come.

Steve Ballmer, a name synonymous with Microsoft's ascendancy, is undeniably one such titan. With a roar of passion and an unyielding determination, Ballmer propelled Microsoft to unimaginable heights during his tenure as CEO.

From his modest beginnings in Detroit to becoming one of the wealthiest and most influential figures in the world, Ballmer's journey is a testament to ambition, innovation, and tenacity.

As we traverse the pages of this book, we will discover the formative experiences that molded Ballmer's character and the events that led him to join the ranks of Microsoft in its early days.

We will explore the unparalleled partnership he formed with Bill Gates and the pivotal role he played in transforming the fledgling company into an empire.

The narrative extends beyond mere corporate success, delving into the essence of Ballmer's leadership style—a mixture of fierce drive, relentless enthusiasm, and occasional controversy. We will witness how he navigated through turbulent times, including the dot-com bubble and the onslaught of competitors, while staying true to his vision.

Chapter 1

A Childhood Shaped by Detroit's Spirit

Early Life and Family Background

In the heart of Detroit, a city known for its indomitable spirit and resilient inhabitants, Steve Ballmer's journey began.

Born on March 24, 1956, he grew up in a modest household that mirrored the blue-collar work ethic deeply ingrained in the city's identity.

Steve's parents, Beatrice and Frederic Ballmer, instilled in him the values of hard work, determination, and perseverance from an early age. Frederic worked as a manager at Ford Motor Company, while Beatrice dedicated herself to raising Steve and his two siblings.

The household was imbued with an atmosphere of intellectual curiosity, as both parents emphasized the importance of education and encouraged their children to pursue their dreams.

Education and Academic Pursuits

Steve's academic prowess soon became apparent as he attended Detroit Country Day School, a prestigious institution known for its rigorous curriculum. He displayed an insatiable thirst for knowledge and an exceptional aptitude for mathematics and technology.

As a teenager, he would often spend countless hours engrossed in computer programming and exploring the burgeoning world of technology.

It was during his high school years that Steve's entrepreneurial spirit began to emerge.

Recognizing the potential of the personal computer revolution, he started his first business venture by developing a traffic analysis program. This early taste of entrepreneurship fueled his ambition and set him on a path that would shape his future.

Developing a Competitive Edge

Steve's academic pursuits took him to Harvard University, where he pursued a degree in applied mathematics and economics. The university provided a fertile ground for intellectual growth and exposed him to diverse ideas and perspectives. At Harvard, Steve's natural leadership abilities came to the forefront, and he excelled not only in his studies but also in his extracurricular activities.

One of the defining moments in Steve's life occurred when he crossed paths with a fellow Harvard student named Bill Gates.

Recognizing their shared passion for technology and business, the two forged a friendship that would prove instrumental in shaping the course of their lives.

Their shared vision of a future dominated by technology and their relentless drive to succeed would lay the foundation for one of the most iconic partnerships in the history of the tech industry.

As Steve Ballmer transitioned from his academic pursuits into the professional world, his competitive edge became increasingly apparent.

He joined Procter & Gamble after graduating from Harvard, where he honed his business acumen and learned valuable lessons about strategy and market dynamics.

This experience would serve as a springboard for the challenges that awaited him in the years to come.

Chapter 2

The Microsoft Connection

Joining the Pioneering Years at Microsoft

As Steve Ballmer completed his tenure at Procter & Gamble, a life-altering opportunity presented itself. In 1980, he received a call from his friend Bill Gates, who had co-founded a small software company called Microsoft.

Gates, recognizing Ballmer's sharp intellect and business acumen, invited him to join the growing team.

Eager to be a part of the burgeoning software industry, Ballmer embraced the offer and joined Microsoft as its 30th employee.

Little did he know that this decision would set him on a path to becoming one of the key figures in the company's history.

In the early years at Microsoft, the company faced numerous challenges and uncertainties. The personal computer revolution was still in its infancy, and the industry was marked by intense competition and rapid technological advancements.

Ballmer, armed with his competitive spirit and unwavering determination, dove headfirst into the challenges that lay ahead.

Rise through the Ranks: From Business Manager to CEO

Steve Ballmer's meteoric rise within Microsoft showcased his innate leadership abilities.

Initially serving as the company's business manager, he quickly proved his worth and took on greater responsibilities. With his keen business sense and strategic acumen, Ballmer played a pivotal role in Microsoft's transformation from a fledgling startup to a global technology powerhouse.

Over the years, Ballmer assumed various roles within the company, including Vice President of Sales and Support, Senior Vice President of Systems Software, and Executive Vice President of Sales and Support.

With each new position, he contributed to the company's growth, solidifying his reputation as a visionary leader.

In 2000, a defining moment arrived when Ballmer succeeded Bill Gates as the Chief Executive Officer (CEO) of Microsoft. As CEO, Ballmer faced the daunting task of steering the company through an era of unprecedented technological change and fierce competition.

His strategic decisions and unwavering commitment to innovation would shape Microsoft's destiny in the years to come.

The Gates-Ballmer Dynamic: Partnership and Challenges

The partnership between Bill Gates and Steve Ballmer was a study in contrasts. Gates, the visionary technologist, and Ballmer, the passionate businessman, complemented each other perfectly. Their dynamic was marked by a shared vision for Microsoft's future, but it was not without its challenges.

As CEO, Ballmer faced the arduous task of navigating the company through legal battles, antitrust investigations, and evolving market dynamics.

The rise of competitors like Apple and Google posed significant challenges to Microsoft's dominance, requiring Ballmer to adapt and innovate to stay ahead.

Despite the challenges, the Gates-Ballmer partnership remained steadfast, with both leaders working in tandem to drive Microsoft's success.

Their collaboration resulted in groundbreaking products such as Windows XP, Xbox, and the Microsoft Office suite, which solidified the company's position as a technology powerhouse.

Chapter 3

Taking the Helm: The Ballmer Era

The Transition to CEO: Vision and Strategy

When Steve Ballmer assumed the role of Chief Executive Officer (CEO) at Microsoft, he faced the immense responsibility of leading one of the world's most influential technology companies. Ballmer wasted no time in setting forth his vision and strategy for the future.

Under his leadership, Microsoft aimed to become a leader in the digital transformation of businesses and individuals. Ballmer recognized the importance of embracing the internet and shifting Microsoft's focus to software and services.

His strategic vision encompassed the idea of a "devices and services" company, which would guide Microsoft's evolution in the years to come.

Navigating the Dot-Com Bubble and Its Aftermath

The turn of the millennium marked a tumultuous period for the technology industry, as the dot-com bubble burst and sent shockwaves throughout the market. As CEO, Ballmer faced the formidable task of navigating Microsoft through these challenging times.

During this era, Ballmer made critical decisions that would shape Microsoft's future. Recognizing the significance of internet technologies, he led the company's initiatives to embrace the internet and transition to a more connected world.

This included the launch of the .NET framework, the introduction of Windows XP, and the integration of web-based services into Microsoft's product portfolio.

Ballmer's resilience and determination in weathering the dot-com bubble's aftermath proved instrumental in ensuring Microsoft's stability and positioning the company for future growth.

Expanding Microsoft's Influence and Product Portfolio

Under Steve Ballmer's leadership, Microsoft experienced a period of significant expansion and diversification.

Ballmer understood the importance of expanding Microsoft's influence beyond its traditional software offerings and exploring new markets.

One of the major milestones during Ballmer's tenure was the introduction of the Microsoft Office Suite, which revolutionized productivity tools and became an integral part of businesses worldwide.

Additionally, Ballmer oversaw the development and launch of the Xbox gaming console, successfully entering the gaming industry and establishing Microsoft as a major player.

Furthermore, Ballmer focused on strategic acquisitions and partnerships to broaden Microsoft's reach. Notable acquisitions during his era included Skype, Yammer, and Nokia's devices and services division. These moves aimed to strengthen Microsoft's position in areas such as communication, social networking, and mobile devices.

Chapter 4

The Passionate Leader

Ballmer's Leadership Style and Corporate Culture.

Throughout his tenure as CEO of Microsoft, Steve Ballmer's leadership style was characterized by his unwavering passion and infectious energy. Known for his enthusiastic and energetic presence, Ballmer fostered a corporate culture that thrived on intensity and collaboration.Ballmer believed in leading by example, often immersing himself in the day-to-day operations of the company. He encouraged a culture of open communication and debate, valuing diverse perspectives and fostering an environment where employees felt empowered to voice their ideas and concerns.

His commitment to transparency and accountability was evident in initiatives such as the "One Microsoft" reorganization, which aimed to break down silos and promote cross-team collaboration. Ballmer's leadership style inspired loyalty and dedication among employees, creating a sense of unity and shared purpose within the company.

Driving Innovation: Windows, Office, and Beyond.

Under Ballmer's guidance, Microsoft continued to drive innovation in its core products, most notably Windows and Office. Ballmer recognized the importance of these flagship products and their ability to shape the future of personal computing.

Windows underwent significant transformations during Ballmer's tenure, with the introduction of Windows XP, Windows Vista, and eventually Windows 7.

These releases showcased Microsoft's commitment to improving user experiences and addressing evolving market demands.

Likewise, Ballmer led the evolution of the Microsoft Office suite, introducing new features and embracing cloud-based services.

This transition allowed Office to remain relevant and competitive in an increasingly interconnected world.

Furthermore, Ballmer recognized the potential of emerging technologies and spearheaded Microsoft's foray into areas such as cloud computing with Azure, artificial intelligence with Cortana, and the hybrid tablet market with the Surface lineup. These strategic moves demonstrated Ballmer's ability to anticipate industry trends and position Microsoft as a leader in transformative technologies.

Challenges and Criticisms: Balancing Vision and Execution.

While Steve Ballmer's tenure as CEO was marked by notable successes, it was not without its challenges and criticisms.

One recurring criticism was Microsoft's perceived slow response to the rise of mobile platforms, particularly Apple's iOS and Google's Android.

Ballmer's focus on maintaining Microsoft's dominance in the traditional PC market led to missed opportunities in the mobile space.

Critics argued that Microsoft failed to adapt quickly enough and lost ground to competitors, impacting its presence in the mobile market. Another area of criticism was Ballmer's ambitious yet sometimes overly optimistic vision for Microsoft's future.

While his enthusiasm was infectious, some questioned the execution and feasibility of certain initiatives.

Examples include the unsuccessful launch of Windows Vista and the acquisition of Nokia's devices and services division, which ultimately led to a write-down of billions of dollars.

However, despite these challenges and criticisms, Ballmer's leadership left an indelible mark on Microsoft's transformation.

His passion, drive, and commitment to innovation laid the groundwork for the company's continued success in the ever-evolving technology landscape.

Chapter 5

A Changing Landscape

Rise of Competitors: Google, Apple, and Open
Source

As Steve Ballmer led Microsoft through the early
2000s, the technology landscape experienced
significant shifts.

New competitors emerged, challenging
Microsoft's dominance and forcing the company to
adapt to a changing market.

One of the primary competitors that gained
prominence during this time was Google. With its
innovative search engine and focus on web-based
services, Google posed a formidable challenge to
Microsoft's traditional software model.

Ballmer recognized the threat and spearheaded initiatives to compete with Google, including the development of the Bing search engine and the expansion of Microsoft's online services.

Another key competitor was Apple, led by the visionary Steve Jobs. Apple's sleek and user-friendly products, such as the iPhone and iPad, revolutionized the consumer electronics industry. Microsoft faced the challenge of catching up in the mobile space and developing products that could rival Apple's offerings.

Additionally, the rise of open-source software, championed by communities like Linux and the Free Software Movement, presented an alternative to Microsoft's proprietary model.

Ballmer navigated the changing dynamics of the industry, acknowledging the significance of open-source software and fostering collaborations with the open-source community.

Strategic Shifts: Cloud Computing and Mobile Revolution

Recognizing the importance of embracing emerging technologies, Steve Ballmer led Microsoft through strategic shifts that would shape the company's future.

One of the most significant transformations was the company's move into cloud computing with the introduction of Microsoft Azure.

Under Ballmer's leadership, Microsoft invested heavily in building its cloud infrastructure and providing cloud-based services to businesses. This shift allowed Microsoft to compete in the rapidly growing market for cloud computing, providing scalable solutions and expanding its presence beyond traditional software offerings.

Furthermore, Ballmer championed Microsoft's entry into the mobile revolution. While Microsoft faced initial challenges in this space, Ballmer spearheaded efforts to develop the Windows Phone platform and establish partnerships with device manufacturers. Despite some setbacks, Microsoft's mobile initiatives demonstrated Ballmer's commitment to adapt and compete in an increasingly mobile-centric world.

Balancing Tradition with Adaptation: Restructuring and Reorganization

As Microsoft faced the evolving landscape of technology, Ballmer recognized the need for organizational restructuring and reorganization. The "One Microsoft" initiative aimed to break down silos within the company and foster collaboration across teams and divisions.

This restructuring allowed Microsoft to streamline operations, improve efficiency, and respond more effectively to market demands.

Moreover, Ballmer led efforts to diversify Microsoft's product portfolio beyond traditional software. The acquisition of companies like Skype and Yammer expanded Microsoft's presence in communication and social networking spaces.

Chapter 6

Ballmer's Legacy and Philanthropic Endeavors

Beyond his role at Microsoft, Steve Ballmer has made a significant impact through his philanthropic endeavors. With a focus on education and community development, Ballmer has dedicated his resources and efforts to improving the lives of others

One of Ballmer's key philanthropic initiatives is his work in education.

Through the Ballmer Group, he supports organizations that strive to provide equal opportunities in education, particularly for underserved communities.

Ballmer understands the transformative power of education and aims to bridge the opportunity gap, ensuring that all individuals have access to quality education and the chance to fulfill their potential.

In addition to education, Ballmer is actively involved in community development. He has contributed to various projects aimed at revitalizing communities and providing resources to those in need.

Through collaborations with local organizations and nonprofits, Ballmer seeks to create positive change and empower communities to thrive.

Ownership of the Los Angeles Clippers: Sports Ventures

Another aspect of Steve Ballmer's post-Microsoft journey is his venture into the world of sports ownership. In 2014, he purchased the Los Angeles Clippers, a professional basketball team in the National Basketball Association (NBA).

Ballmer's ownership of the Clippers brought new energy and enthusiasm to the franchise. He is deeply invested in the team's success, working to create a positive and inclusive culture both on and off the court. Ballmer's leadership has helped the Clippers become a competitive force in the NBA, and he is committed to providing the resources and support necessary for the team's continued growth and success.

Reflecting on Contributions and Lessons Learned

As Steve Ballmer reflects on his contributions and the lessons learned throughout his career, several key themes emerge. One is the importance of embracing change and adaptability.

Ballmer's journey at Microsoft and beyond is marked by his ability to navigate a rapidly evolving industry, recognize emerging trends, and position himself and the organizations he leads for success.

Another valuable lesson is the power of leadership and collaboration. Ballmer's charismatic and energetic leadership style, coupled with his belief in the power of teamwork, has been instrumental in driving innovation and achieving goals. His ability to inspire and unite individuals around a shared vision has been a cornerstone of his success.

Furthermore, Ballmer's commitment to giving back and making a positive impact serves as a reminder of the importance of using one's resources and influence to uplift others.

Through his philanthropic endeavors, Ballmer has sought to create lasting change and improve the lives of individuals and communities.

Chapter 7
Behind the Scenes

Family Life and Relationships

While Steve Ballmer's professional life has been widely known, his personal life and relationships have often remained private. In this chapter, we explore the personal side of Ballmer, including his family life and the relationships that have shaped him.

Ballmer has been married to his wife, Connie Snyder Ballmer, since 1990. Their partnership has been a source of support and strength throughout his career. Together, they have navigated the challenges and successes that come with a life in the public eye.

In addition to his immediate family, Ballmer has forged meaningful relationships with colleagues and mentors throughout his journey.

These connections have played a crucial role in his personal and professional development, providing guidance, support, and valuable insights.

Hobbies and Extracurricular Pursuits

Beyond his professional endeavors, Steve Ballmer has cultivated a range of hobbies and extracurricular interests.

These pursuits offer a glimpse into his multifaceted personality and provide a balance to his demanding professional life. Ballmer has long been known for his enthusiasm for basketball.

His love for the sport extends beyond his ownership of the Los Angeles Clippers, and he can often be found cheering on his favorite teams or engaging in friendly pickup games.

Additionally, Ballmer has shown a passion for the arts and creativity. He has been an advocate for fostering creativity in education and has supported initiatives that promote artistic expression.

His appreciation for the arts extends to his personal life, where he may be found exploring museums, attending performances, or engaging in artistic hobbies.

Balancing Work and Personal Well-being

As a high-profile executive, Steve Ballmer has undoubtedly faced the challenge of balancing the demands of work with his well-being.

He recognizes that personal well-being is fundamental to long-term success and effectiveness.

This may include dedicating time to family, engaging in physical exercise, or pursuing activities that bring him joy and fulfillment. Furthermore, Ballmer has emphasized the value of a supportive network and delegating responsibilities.

By surrounding himself with capable individuals and trusting them to carry out tasks, he has been able to alleviate some of the pressures that come with leadership.

Chapter 8

Lessons from a Trailblazer

Leadership Insights: Tenets of Ballmer's Success

Throughout his career, Steve Ballmer has exemplified key principles and insights that have contributed to his success as a trailblazing leader.

One of the key tenets of Ballmer's success is his unwavering passion and enthusiasm. His infectious energy and dedication to his work have inspired those around him, fostering a culture of commitment and drive.

Ballmer's leadership serves as a testament to the power of passion in motivating teams and driving innovation.

Another critical aspect of Ballmer's leadership is his ability to embrace change and adapt to evolving circumstances.

He recognizes the importance of staying ahead of industry trends, understanding emerging technologies, and anticipating market shifts. By remaining agile and open to new possibilities, Ballmer has positioned himself and his organizations for long-term success.

Additionally, Ballmer places a strong emphasis on teamwork and collaboration.

He understands that diverse perspectives and collective intelligence are essential for solving complex problems and driving meaningful innovation.

Ballmer's leadership style encourages open communication, trust, and a sense of shared purpose, creating an environment where individuals can thrive and contribute their best.

Perseverance and Resilience: Overcoming Adversity

Steve Ballmer's journey has not been without its challenges and setbacks. However, his perseverance and resilience in the face of adversity have been integral to his success.

From the turbulent times of the dot-com bubble to the challenges of entering the mobile market, Ballmer has demonstrated an ability to weather storms and adapt to changing circumstances.

His determination to push forward, learn from failures, and make necessary course corrections has enabled him to overcome obstacles and emerge stronger.

Moreover, Ballmer's resilience extends beyond business challenges. His ability to bounce back from personal setbacks and maintain a positive outlook has played a crucial role in his overall well-being and ability to lead effectively.

Impact on the Tech Industry and Beyond

The impact of Steve Ballmer's contributions extends far beyond Microsoft and the tech industry. Ballmer's tenure at Microsoft witnessed the company's growth into a global powerhouse, shaping the way we interact with technology and transforming industries.

His strategic initiatives, such as the expansion into cloud computing and mobile devices, have had a profound impact on the tech industry's evolution.

Furthermore, Ballmer's philanthropic efforts and commitment to education have left a lasting legacy. Through his contributions, he has sought to create opportunities for individuals and communities to thrive, leaving a positive impact on society as a whole.

Conclusion

Steve Ballmer's Enduring Influence and Legacy

Steve Ballmer's enduring influence and legacy are undeniable. Throughout his career, Ballmer played a pivotal role in shaping the technology industry and driving Microsoft's growth and transformation. From his early days at Microsoft to his tenure as CEO, Ballmer's passion, resilience, and visionary leadership have left an indelible mark on the company and the broader tech landscape.

As a leader, Ballmer exemplified key principles that have become cornerstones of his legacy. His unwavering passion and enthusiasm inspired those around him, fueling a culture of innovation and excellence.

Ballmer's ability to adapt to change and anticipate industry trends allowed Microsoft to navigate through challenging times and seize new opportunities.

Ballmer's impact extends beyond Microsoft and the tech industry. Through his philanthropic endeavors, particularly in education and community development, he has made significant contributions to society, striving to create a more equitable and inclusive world.

Furthermore, his ownership of the Los Angeles Clippers demonstrated his ability to extend his influence beyond technology and pursue ventures in other areas of interest.The lessons learned from Steve Ballmer's journey are invaluable.

His leadership insights, perseverance in the face of adversity, and commitment to making a positive impact serve as inspiration for aspiring leaders and entrepreneurs. Ballmer's legacy is one of resilience, innovation, and a relentless pursuit of excellence.

As we conclude this biography, we reflect on the transformative impact that Steve Ballmer has had on the technology industry, his philanthropic endeavors, and his role as a visionary leader.

Through his unwavering dedication, strategic vision, and commitment to making a difference, Ballmer's influence will continue to shape the world of technology and beyond for years to come.

Printed in Great Britain
by Amazon

41832455R00030